Mike Brownlow

MEET THE PENGUINS

OXFORD
UNIVERSITY PRESS

Please, can we play?

Sorry! Can't stop.
I've got **BIG** things to do.

Please, can we play?

Can't you see
I'm in the middle
of something?

Please, can we play?

No. You might make a mess.

Please, can we play?

Who
said
that?

Please, can we play?

You're
too slow.

Please, can we play?

You don't know the rules.

Please, can we play?

Sssh! I'm trying
to concentrate.
Come back when
I've finished.

Please, can we play?

I'm in a rush!
I've got places to go.

Please, can we . . .

No.

Hmmm, what now?

Please,
can I play?

Yes!

Shall we play with this?

Or how about this?

We could show you
how to do this . . .

or
this . . .

. . . or this!

BRRRP!

And YOU can join in too!

WHEEEE!

WOW!

FANTASTIC!

Please, can *we* play?

We'll think about it.

For Dilly xxx

OXFORD
UNIVERSITY PRESS

Great Clarendon Street, Oxford OX2 6DP

Oxford University Press is a department of the University of Oxford.
It furthers the University's objective of excellence in research, scholarship,
and education by publishing worldwide. Oxford is a registered trade mark of
Oxford University Press in the UK and in certain other countries

British Library Cataloguing in Publication Data available

ISBN: 978-0-19-276867-4

1 3 5 7 9 10 8 6 4 2

Printed in China

Paper used in the production of this book is a natural, recyclable product made
from wood grown in sustainable forests. The manufacturing process conforms
to the environmental regulations of the country of origin